Our Favorite Chicken Recipes

Copyright 2007, Gooseberry Patch
First Printing, April, 2007

Make quick dumplings by cutting flour tortillas into strips and then
cooking them in chicken broth until tender.

Chicken & Dumplings

Serves 4

2 boneless, skinless chicken
    breasts, cut into strips
1/8 t. salt
1/8 t. pepper
1 T. olive oil
2 T. all-purpose flour
14-1/2 oz. can chicken broth
1 c. water

1 onion, sliced
1 c. green beans
1 c. carrots, peeled and
    shredded
2/3 c. biscuit baking mix
1/3 c. cornmeal
1/4 c. shredded Cheddar cheese
1/2 c. milk

Sprinkle chicken with salt and pepper. Heat oil in a skillet over
medium heat; cook chicken until golden. Sprinkle with flour; stir in
broth, water, onion, beans and carrots. Bring to a boil; reduce heat and
simmer for 5 minutes. In a bowl, combine baking mix, cornmeal and
cheese; stir in milk. Drop by tablespoonfuls into soup; return to a boil.
Simmer, covered, for 10 to 12 minutes.

Fill a basket with the fixin's for a simple supper like Super-Easy Chicken & Noodles and deliver to new parents...how thoughtful!

Super-Easy Chicken & Noodles

Serves 4

1 lb. boneless, skinless chicken
    breasts, cubed
1 T. oil
10-3/4 oz. can cream of chicken
    soup

1/2 c. milk
1/8 t. pepper
3 c. cooked medium egg noodles
1/3 c. grated Parmesan cheese

In a large skillet over medium heat, cook chicken in oil for 10 to
15 minutes, until golden. Stir in remaining ingredients; heat through.

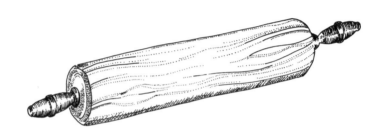

Flatten chicken between wax paper using a rolling pin and a little muscle...just toss the paper and there's no mess!

Smothered Chicken

Serves 4

4 boneless, skinless chicken
    breasts
garlic powder to taste
1 T. oil
4-oz. can sliced mushrooms,
    drained

1 c. shredded Mexican-blend
    cheese
1/2 c. bacon bits
1/2 c. green onion, chopped

Flatten chicken to 1/4-inch thickness; sprinkle with garlic powder.
Heat oil in a large skillet over medium heat; sauté chicken for
4 minutes per side, until golden. Top chicken with remaining
ingredients. Reduce heat, cover and cook until chicken juices run
clear and cheese is melted.

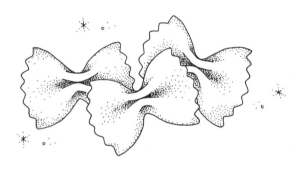

Try other flavored pasta in place of the spaghetti in this dish...there are so many to choose from! Try pasta flavored with spinach, garlic, basil or even spicy red peppers.

Chicken Spaghetti

Serves 4

1/4 to 1/2 c. butter
1 lb. boneless, skinless chicken
    breasts, cut into bite-size
    pieces
1 onion, chopped
8-oz. can sliced mushrooms,
    drained

16-oz. pkg. broccoli flowerets
1 clove garlic, minced
salt and pepper to taste
16-oz. pkg. spaghetti, cooked
Garnish: grated Parmesan
    cheese

Melt butter in a large skillet over medium heat. Add chicken and cook until lightly golden. Add onion, mushrooms, broccoli and garlic; sauté until chicken is cooked through and vegetables are tender. Sprinkle with salt and pepper; toss with cooked spaghetti. Garnish with Parmesan cheese.

Freeze chicken breasts in their marinades in airtight containers. By the time it's frozen and thawed for cooking, the meat will have absorbed just enough flavor...so easy and delicious!

Mediterranean Roast Chicken

Serves 6

14-1/2 oz. can diced tomatoes
  with roasted garlic and
  onions
6-oz. jar quartered artichokes,
  drained

1/3 c. pitted Kalamata olives
3 to 4-lb. deli roast chicken
1/2 c. crumbled feta cheese

Combine tomatoes, artichokes and olives in a small saucepan over medium heat; bring to a boil. Simmer for one minute. Carve chicken into serving pieces. Spoon sauce over chicken; sprinkle with feta cheese.

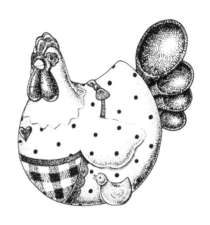

Before marinating chicken, pour some marinade into a plastic
squeeze bottle for easy basting...how clever!

Tarragon Chicken

4 to 6 boneless, skinless
   chicken breasts
salt and pepper to taste
1/2 c. all-purpose flour, divided
1/4 c. butter
1 to 2 T. onion, chopped

1/4 c. white wine or chicken
   broth
1 T. fresh tarragon, chopped
1/2 c. chicken broth
1/4 c. whipping cream

Rub chicken with salt and pepper. Dredge in 1/4 cup flour, reserving remaining flour; set aside. Melt butter in a skillet over medium heat add chicken. Cook chicken on both sides until golden; remove from skillet and keep warm. Stir in onion; sauté until translucent. Pour in wine or chicken broth; cook until bubbly. Add remaining flour; sprinkle with tarragon. Stir in chicken broth until smooth; return chicken to skillet. Cook until heated through; stir in cream.

Grilling bone-in chicken? Rub any dry spices under the skin if desired but leave the skin on while cooking...it keeps moisture in. Also, wait until the last few minutes of cooking time to brush on sauces for the best flavor.

Chicken Piccata

1/4 c. plus 2 T. all-purpose flour, divided
2 T. chicken bouillon granules, divided
4 boneless, skinless chicken breasts
2 T. olive oil
1 T. butter
1/2 c. white wine or chicken broth
1/4 c. lemon juice
2 T. water
2 T. capers, drained and rinsed
2 T. fresh parsley, chopped

Combine 1/4 cup flour and 1/2 teaspoon bouillon granules; set aside. Place chicken between 2 sheets of wax paper and flatten to 1/4-inch thickness. Dip chicken in flour mixture to coat. Heat oil in a large skillet over medium heat; cook chicken 4 to 5 minutes on each side, or until cooked through. Remove chicken and keep warm. Melt butter in skillet and add remaining flour, scraping up browned bits. Add wine or broth, lemon juice, water and remaining bouillon granules; simmer for 2 minutes. Stir in capers and parsley. Spoon sauce over chicken.

Freezing cooked rice makes for quick-fix meals later.
Use it for stir-fry dishes, casseroles, or mix in fresh
vegetables for an easy side dish...just freeze servings
in flat plastic zipping bags.

Braised Chicken Breast

Serves 4 to 6

1 c. all-purpose flour
salt and pepper to taste
4 to 6 boneless, skinless
    chicken breasts
2 to 4 T. butter
1/2 c. onion, diced
1 c. sliced mushrooms

8-oz. can diced tomatoes
1/2 c. chicken broth
2 T. mustard
1 c. whipping cream
Garnish: chopped fresh parsley,
cooked rice

Combine flour, salt and pepper; coat chicken, shaking off excess. Melt butter over medium heat in a large skillet; add chicken. Cook chicken until golden. Add onion and mushrooms; cook until tender. Add diced tomatoes, chicken broth and mustard; mix well. Simmer over low heat for 20 to 30 minutes. Stir in whipping cream; heat through. Garnish with chopped parsley. Serve over rice.

Serve fried chicken in clean new paper buckets from the local paint store. Lined with red-checked paper napkins just for fun, they're easy to toss when the picnic is over!

Country-Fried Chicken

Serves 4 to 6

1 c. all-purpose flour
1 t. salt
1 t. pepper
1 t. garlic salt
1 t. poultry seasoning

1 c. milk
1 egg, beaten
3 to 4 lbs. chicken
2 c. oil

Mix together flour, salt, pepper, garlic salt and poultry seasoning in a bowl; set aside. Blend together milk and egg in another bowl. Dip chicken in milk mixture; coat with flour mixture. Heat oil in a large skillet over medium heat; fry chicken pieces until golden on both sides. Reduce heat and cook for an additional 20 to 30 minutes, until chicken is cooked through.

Make a delicious honey-mustard dip for chicken nuggets with
2/3 cup honey and 1/3 cup mustard. Try different kinds of honey
and mustard to create flavor variations.

Crunchy Ranch Chicken

Serves 6

8-1/2 oz. pkg. cornbread
   muffin mix
1-oz. pkg. ranch salad
   dressing mix

1 c. milk
6 boneless, skinless chicken
   breasts
2 T. oil

Combine cornbread mix and salad dressing mix in a large plastic zipping bag; set aside. Pour milk into a shallow bowl. Dip chicken into milk; place in cornbread mixture and shake to coat. Heat oil in a large skillet over medium heat. Add chicken; cook until golden on both sides, about 6 to 7 minutes per side, or until juices run clear.

Pick up a roast chicken at the deli for 2 easy
meals in one. Serve it hot the first night, then slice
or cube the rest to become the delicious start of a
salad, soup or sandwich supper the next.

Cranberry Chicken

Serves 4

4 slices bacon
4 boneless, skinless chicken
    breasts
10-oz. jar pearl onions, drained
1-1/2 oz. pkg. onion soup mix

16-oz. can whole-berry
    cranberry sauce
1/3 c. water
1/4 t. dried thyme

Cook bacon until crisp; crumble and set aside. Reserve drippings in skillet. Brown chicken in same skillet; remove from heat. Combine remaining ingredients; mix well. Pour over chicken; simmer, covered, for 40 minutes, or until juices run clear when pierced with a fork.

Be sure to wash hands, countertops, cutting boards and knives with soapy water after handling raw chicken.

Balsamic Chicken & Pears

Serves 4

2 t. oil, divided
4 boneless, skinless chicken
   breasts
2 Bosc pears, cored and cut into
   8 wedges

1 c. chicken broth
3 T. balsamic vinegar
2 t. cornstarch
1-1/2 t. sugar
1/4 c. dried cherries or raisins

Heat one teaspoon oil in a large non-stick skillet over medium-high heat; add chicken. Cook until golden and cooked through, about 4 to 5 minutes per side. Transfer to a plate; keep warm. Heat remaining oil in same skillet; add pears and cook until tender and golden. In a small bowl, combine remaining ingredients except cherries or raisins. Stir broth mixture into skillet with pears; add cherries or raisins. Bring to a boil over medium heat; cook for one minute, stirring constantly. Return chicken to pan; heat through.

Create a cozy Italian restaurant feel for your next pasta dinner. Toss a red & white checked tablecloth over the table, light drip candles in empty bottles and add a basket of garlic bread.

Creamy Chicken Italiano

Serves 6

2 16-oz. jars Alfredo sauce
15-oz. can mixed vegetables,
    drained
12-oz. can chicken, drained
1/2 t. Italian seasoning

1/2 t. salt
1/4 t. pepper
1/4 t. hot pepper sauce
16-oz. pkg. rotini pasta, cooked
1 c. shredded mozzarella cheese

Combine all ingredients except pasta and cheese in a large saucepan
over medium heat; mix well. Simmer for 5 minutes. Add rotini, tossing
to coat. Reduce heat to low. Sprinkle with cheese; heat until cheese
is melted.

Don't forget about prepared Alfredo sauce in a jar when time
is really short! Mix cooked chicken, pasta and veggies together
in a saucepan and top it off with ready-made sauce...heat
through and dinner's done.

Chicken & Broccoli Alfredo ~~Sauce~~ *Serves 4*

COUNTRY GRAVY

8-oz. pkg. linguine pasta,
   uncooked
1 c. broccoli flowerets
2 T. butter
1 lb. boneless, skinless chicken
   breasts, cubed

10-3/4 oz. ~~can cream of~~ *OR*
   ~~mushroom soup~~
~~1/2 c. milk~~
1/2 c. grated Parmesan cheese
1/4 t. pepper

Cook linguine according to package directions; add broccoli during the last 4 minutes of cooking time. Drain; set aside. Heat butter in a large skillet over medium heat; add chicken. Cook until juices run clear when pierced with a fork; reduce heat. Stir in soup, milk, cheese, pepper and linguine mixture; heat through.

Shake up a traditional dish for a change of pace. Use fettuccine
or angel hair pasta in Chicken Tetrazzini...try rotini or
wagon wheel pasta in macaroni & cheese.

Chicken Tetrazzini

3 T. butter
1 onion, chopped
1/4 c. celery, chopped
2 c. cooked chicken, diced
10-3/4 oz. can cream of
    mushroom soup
2-1/2 c. chicken broth

1 t. lemon juice
1/4 t. pepper
1/8 t. nutmeg
6-oz. pkg. spaghetti, uncooked
    and coarsely broken
4-oz. can sliced mushrooms,
    drained

Melt butter in a large soup pot over medium heat. Sauté onion and celery until tender. Stir in chicken, soup, broth, lemon juice, pepper and nutmeg; add spaghetti. Bring to a boil; reduce heat and simmer for 15 minutes, or until spaghetti is tender. Add mushrooms; cook until mushrooms are heated through.

Sauté chicken pieces in a skillet without overcrowding them and the result will be juicy, tender chicken with a crispy crust.

Chicken Crunch Supreme

Serves 4 to 6

2 c. cooked chicken, cubed
1/4 c. celery, diced
1 t. dried, minced onion
10-3/4 oz. can cream of
    mushroom soup
1-1/2 c. cooked thin
    egg noodles
1 c. shredded Cheddar cheese

1/3 c. mayonnaise
8-oz. can sliced water
    chestnuts, drained
salt and pepper to taste
2 c. corn flake cereal, crushed
1/3 c. sliced almonds
1/4 c. butter, melted

Mix together chicken, celery, onion, soup, noodles, cheese, mayonnaise, water chestnuts, salt and pepper; spread in an ungreased 9"x9" baking pan. Top with cereal and almonds; drizzle with butter. Bake, covered, at 375 degrees for 50 minutes; uncover and bake for an additional 10 minutes.

When simmering chicken, toss in a cube or 2 of chicken bouillon.
Save the broth and it will make a delicious soup or gravy!

Southern Fried Chicken & Fritters

2 eggs, beaten
2 T. milk
1 c. bread crumbs

1-1/2 lbs. boneless, skinless
chicken breasts, cubed
oil for deep frying

Whisk eggs and milk together in a shallow bowl; set aside. Place bread crumbs in a pie plate; set aside. Dip chicken in egg mixture; coat with bread crumbs. Reserve remaining egg mixture. Add oil to cover a large skillet; heat over medium heat until hot. Add chicken; cover and cook for 15 minutes. Uncover and flip chicken; cook until juices run clear when pierced with a fork. Remove to plate; keep warm. Blend remaining egg mixture and bread crumbs together; add additional milk or beaten egg to make a thick paste. Drop by tablespoonfuls into same skillet and cook until golden on both sides, about 5 minutes; drain. Serve chicken and fritters together.

Pick up a disposable roasting pan when preparing a big dinner.
Afterwards, just toss it away...no mess to clean up!

Oven Barbecued Chicken

Serves 6 to 8

3 to 4 lbs. boneless, skinless
    chicken breasts, cubed
1/2 c. margarine, melted

5-1/2 oz. pkg. barbecue potato
    chips, crushed
garlic powder to taste

Dip chicken in margarine; roll in chips and sprinkle with garlic powder. Arrange on a baking sheet that has been lightly sprayed with non-stick vegetable spray. Bake, uncovered, at 350 degrees for one hour.

Homemade chicken broth is delicious and easy with a slow cooker. Combine 6 chicken thighs with some chopped carrots, celery and onion. Top with 6 cups water, cover and cook on low setting for 8 to 10 hours. Strain broth, refrigerate and skim fat. The cooked chicken is delicious in soups and salads.

Sunday Chicken & Dressing

Serves 12

10-3/4 oz. can cream of
    chicken soup
10-3/4 oz. can cream of celery
    or cream of mushroom soup
1 c. chicken broth

2-1/2 to 3 lbs. cooked chicken,
    cubed
2 6-oz. pkgs. chicken-flavored
    stuffing mix, prepared

Combine soups and broth in a bowl; set aside. Place half of chicken
in a lightly greased 13"x9" baking pan; top with half each of stuffing
and soup mixture. Repeat layers, ending with soup mixture. Bake at
350 degrees for one hour.

Fresh out of croutons for this crunchy topping? Use herb-flavored stuffing mix in their place and it'll be just as yummy!

Chicken Divan

Serves 6 to 8

2 10-oz. pkgs. frozen broccoli,
   cooked
2 c. cooked chicken, sliced
2 10-3/4 oz. cans cream of
   chicken soup
1 c. mayonnaise

1 t. lemon juice
1/2 t. curry powder
1-1/2 c. shredded Cheddar
   cheese
1/2 c. croutons, crushed

Arrange broccoli in a lightly greased 13"x9" baking pan; top with chicken. Combine soup, mayonnaise, lemon juice and curry powder in a bowl. Pour over chicken; sprinkle with cheese and croutons. Bake, uncovered, at 325 degrees for 30 minutes.

When roasting a chicken, keep the breast from drying out by tenting it with aluminum foil. Remove during last 30 minutes of roasting time to allow the skin to brown properly.

Spicy Sausage & Chicken Creole

Serves 4

14-1/2 oz. can diced tomatoes
1/2 c. long-cooking rice, uncooked
1/2 c. hot water
2 t. hot pepper sauce
1/4 t. garlic powder
1/4 t. dried oregano

16-oz. pkg. frozen broccoli, corn & red pepper blend, thawed
4 boneless, skinless chicken thighs
1/2 lb. Italian pork sausage links, cooked and quartered
8-oz. can tomato sauce

Combine tomatoes, rice, water, hot sauce and seasonings in an ungreased 13"x9" baking pan. Cover and bake at 375 degrees for 10 minutes. Stir vegetables into tomato mixture; top with chicken and sausage. Pour tomato sauce over top. Bake, covered, at 375 degrees for 40 minutes, or until juices of chicken run clear.

To peel garlic easily, crush the clove with the side of a knife.
For really speedy mincing, use a garlic press.

Chicken Scampi

Serves 2 to 3

4 to 6 cloves garlic, minced
2 T. fresh parsley, chopped
2 T. lemon juice
1/4 c. white wine or chicken
    broth
1/2 c. olive oil
1/2 t. salt
1 t. garlic powder
1 t. dried oregano
1/4 c. chili sauce
2 boneless, skinless chicken
    breasts, diced
cooked angel hair pasta
Garnish: grated Romano cheese

Combine all ingredients except pasta and Romano cheese in a lightly greased 13"x9" baking pan. Bake, uncovered, at 450 degrees for 15 to 20 minutes. Serve over pasta; garnish with cheese.

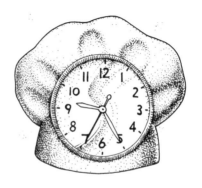

Let roasted chicken rest for 10 to 15 minutes before carving to allow juices to be distributed throughout the meat. Standing the chicken up allows more juices to run into the drier breast area.

Lemon-Pepper Chicken

Serves 4 to 6

2 T. lemon-pepper seasoning
1 T. seasoned salt
1-1/2 t. garlic salt
3 T. butter
1/4 c. olive oil

4 to 6 boneless, skinless
   chicken breasts
1 c. all-purpose flour
1/2 c. lemon juice
1/2 c. water

Mix together seasonings and set aside. Melt butter in a skillet over medium heat; add olive oil. Pat chicken dry; roll in flour. Add chicken to skillet and cook until golden on one side; sprinkle with half of seasoning mixture. Turn chicken; sprinkle on other side with remaining seasoning. Continue cooking until crusty and golden on both sides. Add lemon juice and water to skillet and simmer for 10 minutes. Arrange chicken in a lightly greased 13"x9" baking pan; spoon pan juices over top. Bake, uncovered, at 325 degrees for 45 minutes.

There are so many great-tasting cream soups...mushroom, celery, onion and chicken. Shake up an old favorite recipe by trying a different one each time!

Company Chicken

Serves 4

8 slices Canadian bacon
4 boneless, skinless chicken
    breasts
10-3/4 oz. can cream of
    mushroom soup

8-oz. container sour cream
Garnish: green onions, chopped

Place bacon in a greased 13"x9" baking pan; arrange chicken breasts
on top. Bake at 350 degrees for 30 minutes. Combine soup and sour
cream; spread over chicken. Continue baking for an additional
30 minutes. Garnish with onions.

There is nothing better on a cold wintry day than a properly made pot pie.

-Craig Claiborne

Chicken Pot Pie

Serves 4 to 6

2 c. cooked chicken, chopped
15-oz. can mixed vegetables,
    drained
2 10-3/4 oz. cans cream of
    chicken soup

1 c. milk
10-oz. tube refrigerated
    biscuits, quartered

Combine first 4 ingredients together; place in an ungreased 3-quart casserole dish. Bake at 400 degrees for 20 minutes. Arrange biscuit pieces on top of hot chicken mixture; bake, uncovered, until golden, about 15 minutes.

When frying or browning chicken, use a non-stick skillet, which requires less added fat, or use a skillet with fat-free non-stick vegetable spray to reduce the amount of fat used.

Cheesy Chicken & Mac

Serves 6 to 8

2 c. cooked chicken, diced
2 c. elbow macaroni, uncooked
2 c. milk
2 10-3/4 oz. cans cream of
   mushroom soup

2 onions, diced
8-oz. pkg. pasteurized process
   cheese spread, diced

Combine all ingredients; spread in an ungreased 13"x9" baking pan. Cover and refrigerate overnight. Bake, uncovered, at 350 degrees for one hour.

Juicy Buttermilk Chicken is ideal for taking along on a hike and picnic. Wrapped in wax paper, it tucks nicely into a pail along with some fresh fruit and homemade rolls.

Buttermilk Chicken

Serves 4 to 6

1-1/2 c. buttermilk, divided
3/4 c. all-purpose flour
1-1/2 t. salt
1/2 t. pepper
2-1/2 lbs. boneless, skinless
    chicken breasts, cubed

1/4 c. margarine, melted
10-3/4 oz. can cream of chicken
    soup

Pour 1/4 cup buttermilk in a bowl; set aside. Combine flour, salt
and pepper in another bowl. Dip chicken into buttermilk, then coat
with flour mixture; set aside. Pour margarine into an ungreased
13"x9" baking pan; arrange chicken in pan. Bake at 375 degrees
for 30 minutes. Turn chicken over; bake for an additional 15 minutes.
Blend remaining buttermilk with soup; pour over chicken. Bake for
15 minutes, or until chicken is tender.

Here's an easy sauce that's just right spooned over
Bacon-Wrapped Chicken. Melt a tablespoon of butter and
stir in 3 tablespoons Dijon or honey mustard...sweet,
tangy and oh-so good.

Bacon-Wrapped Chicken

Serves 2

2 boneless, skinless chicken
  breasts
2 T. chive and onion-flavored
  cream cheese, softened and
  divided

2 T. butter, divided
salt and pepper to taste
dried tarragon to taste
2 slices bacon

Flatten chicken to 1/2-inch thickness; spread one tablespoon cream cheese over each chicken breast. Top each with one tablespoon butter, salt, pepper and tarragon. Roll up chicken; wrap one slice bacon around each chicken breast; secure with a toothpick. Place seam-side down in a lightly greased 8"x8" baking pan. Bake at 400 degrees for 25 minutes, or until juices run clear when pierced with a fork.

To bring out the best taste in chicken or veggies for Mexican recipes, grill them on an outdoor grill. The flavor will really shine through.

Fiesta Chicken Bake

Serves 4 to 6

4 to 6 boneless, skinless
   chicken breasts, cooked
2 10-3/4 oz. cans cream of
   chicken soup

16-oz. container sour cream
10-oz. can tomatoes with chiles
1-1/2 c. shredded Monterey Jack
   cheese

Arrange chicken in an ungreased 13"x9" baking pan. Mix together
remaining ingredients; spread over chicken. Bake at 350 degrees for
25 to 30 minutes.

Why not pack a picnic tin with hearty food and sweet treats, then deliver to a local firehouse? What a welcome surprise!

Firehouse Chicken

1 lb. chicken cutlets
2 c. dry bread crumbs
2 t. dried parsley
1/2 c. grated Parmesan cheese
1/2 lb. sliced mozzarella cheese
10-3/4 oz. can cream of
    chicken soup

3 T. mayonnaise
3/4 c. water
3/4 c. shredded mozzarella
    cheese

Flatten cutlets to 1/4-inch thickness; coat with bread crumbs. Sprinkle with parsley and Parmesan cheese. Place mozzarella slice in the center of each cutlet. Roll up, secure with a toothpick and arrange in a greased 13"x9" baking pan. Combine soup, mayonnaise and water in a bowl. Pour over cutlets and top with shredded mozzarella. Bake at 375 degrees for one hour.

Clean up's a snap when baking pans are lined
with foil before adding the chicken.

Mother's Roasted Chicken

Serves 4

1 t. paprika
1/2 t. onion powder
1/4 t. garlic powder
1/2 t. dried thyme

1 to 2 t. salt
3/4 t. pepper
3-lb. roasting chicken
1 c. onion, chopped

Combine seasonings and rub on outside of chicken; place in a
plastic zipping bag and refrigerate overnight. Remove chicken from
bag. Place onion inside chicken; place chicken in a lightly greased
13"x9" baking pan. Bake, uncovered, at 350 degrees for one hour and
15 minutes, or until juices run clear.

Pick up prepared stuffing in the meat section at your grocer.
It's ready to bake...you just top chicken breasts or spoon
alongside a turkey breast!

Bruschetta Chicken Bake

Serves 6

14-1/2 oz. can diced tomatoes
6-oz. pkg. herb-flavored
    stuffing mix
1/2 c. water

1-1/2 lbs. boneless, skinless
    chicken breasts, cubed
1 c. shredded mozzarella cheese

Combine tomatoes, stuffing mix and water in a medium bowl.
Stir just until moistened; set aside. Arrange chicken in a lightly
greased 13"x9" baking pan; sprinkle with cheese. Top with stuffing
mixture. Bake, uncovered, at 400 degrees for 20 to 25 minutes, until
chicken is cooked through.

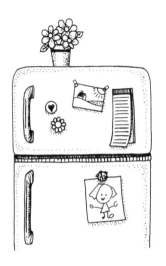

Not able to use chicken within 2 days of purchasing?
No problem! Properly packaged, chicken can be frozen and
will maintain top quality for up to one year.

Chicken-Asparagus Casserole

Serves 4 to 6

8-oz. pkg. pasteurized process
    cheese spread, diced
10-3/4 oz. can cream of
    mushroom soup
1 c. cooked chicken, cubed

2-oz. jar diced pimentos,
    drained
15-oz. can asparagus, drained
3/4 c. saltine crackers, crushed
2 t. butter, diced

Combine cheese and soup in a saucepan over low heat. Cook until
cheese is melted, about 6 to 8 minutes. Stir in chicken and pimentos.
Spread mixture in an ungreased 2-quart casserole dish; arrange
asparagus over top. Sprinkle cracker crumbs over asparagus and dot
with butter. Bake at 350 degrees until golden, about 20 to 25 minutes.

Root vegetables like potatoes, carrots and onions grow tender and sweet with all-day slow cooking. Give sweet potatoes and parsnips a try too...delicious!

Savory Chicken & Potatoes

Serves 4 to 6

1 onion, thinly sliced
4 to 5 potatoes, peeled and
    cubed
4 to 6 boneless, skinless
    chicken breasts

10-3/4 oz. can golden
    mushroom soup
1/2 t. dried marjoram

Arrange onion slices in a slow cooker; add potatoes, then chicken.
Spread soup over top; sprinkle with marjoram. Cover and cook on
low setting for 7 to 8 hours, until chicken and potatoes are tender.

Try not to peek! It's hard, when the food just smells
so good, but cooking time increases by 15 to 20 minutes
every time a slow cooker's lid is lifted.

Sunshine Chicken

Serves 6

6 boneless, skinless chicken
    breasts
1/4 c. molasses
2 T. cider vinegar

2 T. Worcestershire sauce
2 T. orange juice
2 t. Dijon mustard
1/8 to 1/4 t. hot pepper sauce

Arrange chicken in a slow cooker; set aside. Combine remaining
ingredients and brush over chicken. Cover and cook on low setting
for 7 to 9 hours, or on high setting for 3 to 4 hours.

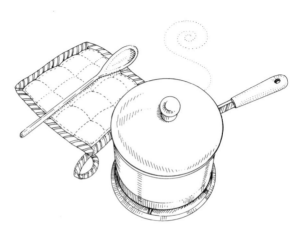

Cook up a big pot of chicken to freeze for later.
For juicy, flavorful chicken, cover with water and simmer
gently just until tender, then turn off the heat and let the
chicken cool in its own broth.

Aloha Chicken

4 lbs. boneless, skinless chicken
20-oz. can pineapple chunks
11-oz. can mandarin oranges, drained
1 green or red pepper, chopped
1/4 c. onion, chopped
1 clove garlic, minced
1 T. soy sauce
1 t. fresh ginger, peeled and grated

Arrange chicken in a slow cooker; set aside. Combine remaining ingredients; pour over chicken. Cover and cook on low setting for 8 to 10 hours.

Make gravy after a slow-cooked chicken is done...it's easy. Set aside chicken, leaving juices in the slow cooker. Stir up a smooth paste of 1/4 cup cold water and 1/4 cup cornstarch. Pour into slow cooker, stir well and set on high. In about 15 minutes, gravy will come to a boil...it's ready to serve!

Lemony "Baked" Chicken

3 to 4-lb. chicken
2 T. olive oil
1 lemon, quartered

2 cloves garlic, minced
1 t. dried parsley
salt and pepper to taste

Pat chicken dry with paper towel; rub with oil. Put lemon inside chicken; place in a slow cooker. Sprinkle with garlic, parsley, salt and pepper. Cover and cook on high setting for one hour. Turn to low setting and cook for an additional 6 to 7 hours.

For the juiciest chicken, slip a quartered orange or
apple inside while roasting.

Grandma's Garlic Chicken

Serves 6 to 8

6 to 8 boneless, skinless
    chicken breasts
4 c. water
16-oz. bottle Italian salad
    dressing
1/4 c. onion, diced

1/4 c. soy sauce
2 T. oil
2 T. lemon juice
2 T. dried parsley
1 T. garlic, minced

Combine all ingredients in a large plastic zipping bag; refrigerate
overnight. Transfer chicken and marinade to a slow cooker. Cover and
cook on low setting for 4 hours. Increase to high setting and cook
for an additional 2 hours, or until chicken juices run clear.

Early American homes always had a kettle of savory stew bubbling at the back of the fireplace. With a slow cooker on your kitchen counter, you can cook up the same delicious slow-simmered flavor!

Slow-Cooker Chicken Stew

Serves 4

2 boneless, skinless chicken
    breasts, cubed
1/2 to 1 t. Greek seasoning
2 onions, chopped
16-oz. pkg. baby carrots

6 potatoes, cubed
4-oz. can sliced mushrooms
2 10-3/4 oz. cans cream of
    mushroom soup

Sprinkle chicken breasts with Greek seasoning; arrange in a slow
cooker. Add onions, carrots, potatoes and mushrooms with liquid;
cover and cook on high setting for 2 hours. Reduce to low setting
and cook for an additional 5 to 6 hours.

Add a tasty crunchy topping to slow-cooked casseroles...
try finely crushed cheese crackers, herbed stuffing mix or
even barbecue potato chips!

Sticky Chicken

Serves 4 to 6

2 t. paprika
1 t. cayenne pepper
1/2 t. garlic powder
1 t. onion powder
1 t. dried thyme

1 t. white pepper
4 t. salt
1/2 t. pepper
3 to 4-lb. chicken
1 c. onion, chopped

Mix together first 8 ingredients; set aside. Remove and discard skin from chicken; rub with spice mixture. Place chicken in a plastic zipping bag and refrigerate overnight. Remove chicken from bag. Sprinkle onion in a slow cooker; place chicken on top. Cover and cook on low setting for 8 hours.

Look for inexpensive Asian-themed plates, bowls and teacups at an import store. They'll make even the simplest Oriental meals special. Don't forget the fortune cookies!

Orange Teriyaki Chicken

Serves 4 to 6

1-1/2 c. chicken broth
1/2 c. teriyaki sauce
1/2 c. green onion, sliced and
    divided
3 cloves garlic, minced
3/4 c. orange marmalade

2 T. cornstarch
8 boneless, skinless chicken
    thighs
cooked rice
Garnish: 1/2 c. chopped walnuts

Mix broth, sauce, 1/4 cup onion, garlic, marmalade and cornstarch in a slow cooker. Add chicken; turn to coat. Cover and cook on low setting for 8 to 9 hours. Serve over rice, garnished with walnuts and remaining onion.

Keep tiny pots of fresh herbs on the kitchen windowsill...they'll be
right at your fingertips for any recipe!

Rosemary & Thyme Chicken

Serves 4

3-lb. chicken
1 to 2 T. garlic, minced
kosher salt to taste
1/2 onion, sliced into wedges

4 sprigs fresh rosemary
3 sprigs fresh thyme
seasoning salt to taste

Rub inside of chicken with garlic and kosher salt. Stuff with onion
wedges and herb sprigs. Sprinkle seasoning salt on outside of chicken;
place in slow cooker. Cover and cook on low setting for 8 to 10 hours.

Make a fresh-tasting side dish for Coq Au Vin.
Combine 3 to 4 sliced zucchini, 1/2 teaspoon minced
garlic and a tablespoon of chopped fresh basil.
Sauté in a little olive oil until tender.

Coq Au Vin

4 boneless, skinless chicken
    breasts
16-oz. pkg. sliced mushrooms
15-oz. jar pearl onions, drained
1/2 c. dry white wine or
    chicken broth
1 t. dried thyme
1 bay leaf
1 c. chicken broth
1/3 c. all-purpose flour
cooked rice
Garnish: fresh parsley, chopped

Place chicken in a slow cooker; top with mushrooms and onions.
Drizzle with wine or broth and sprinkle with thyme; add bay leaf.
Stir together broth and flour; pour into slow cooker. Cover and cook
on low setting for 5 hours, until chicken juices run clear. Discard bay
leaf. Serve over rice; sprinkle with parsley.

Layer slices of leftover roast chicken over stuffing or mashed potatoes, ladle gravy over the top and freeze... perfect for lunches or dinners on the go. Just microwave for a few minutes, until piping hot.

Maple Praline Chicken

Serves 6

6 boneless, skinless chicken
    breasts
2 T. Cajun seasoning
1/4 c. butter, melted
1/2 c. maple syrup

2 T. brown sugar, packed
1 c. chopped pecans
6-oz. pkg. long-grain and wild
    rice, cooked

Sprinkle chicken with Cajun seasoning. In a skillet over medium-high heat, cook chicken in butter until golden. Arrange chicken in a slow cooker. Mix together syrup, brown sugar and pecans; pour over chicken. Cover and cook on low setting for 6 to 8 hours. Serve with cooked rice.

Cook a double batch of rice, then freeze half in a plastic
freezer bag for another meal. When you're ready to use
the frozen rice, just microwave on high for one minute per
cup to thaw, 2 to 3 minutes per cup to warm it through.
Fluff with a fork...ready to use!

Jammin' Jambalaya

Serves 10 to 12

1 lb. boneless, skinless chicken
    breasts, cubed
1 lb. andouille sausage, sliced
28-oz. can diced tomatoes
1 onion, chopped
1 green pepper, chopped
1 c. celery, chopped
1 c. chicken broth

2 t. Cajun seasoning
2 t. dried oregano
2 t. dried parsley
1 t. cayenne pepper
1/2 t. dried thyme
1 lb. frozen cooked shrimp,
    thawed and tails removed
cooked rice

Place chicken, sausage, tomatoes, onion, pepper, celery and broth in a slow cooker. Stir in seasonings; mix well. Cover and cook for 7 to 8 hours on low setting, or 3 to 4 hours on high setting. Add shrimp during final 30 minutes of cooking time. Serve over cooked rice.

To shred cooked chicken, use two forks and insert the prongs,
back sides facing each other, into the center of a portion of meat.
Then simply pull the forks gently away from each other.

Southwest Slow-Cooker Chicken

Serves 4 to 6

15-oz. can corn, drained and
    divided
16-oz. can black beans, drained,
    rinsed and divided
16-oz. jar mild salsa, divided
4 boneless, skinless chicken
    breasts

Garnish: shredded cheese, sour
    cream, sliced green onion,
    chopped red and yellow
    peppers

Layer three-quarters of the corn and beans and half the salsa in a
slow cooker. Arrange chicken over salsa; top with remaining corn,
beans and salsa. Cover and cook on low setting for 8 hours. Remove
chicken and shred; stir back into slow-cooker mixture. Add desired
garnishes just before serving.

Slow-cook a double batch of chicken...shred leftovers for
scrumptious, quick & easy tacos and burritos.

Chicken Cordon Bleu

4 to 6 boneless, skinless
   chicken breasts
4 to 6 thin slices deli ham
4 to 6 slices Swiss cheese

10-3/4 oz. can cream of
   mushroom soup
1/4 c. milk

Place each chicken breast in a plastic zipping bag. Flatten to 1/4-inch thick; remove from bag. Top each with a slice of ham and a slice of cheese; roll up and secure with a toothpick. Arrange rolls in a slow cooker in layers. Mix together soup and milk; pour over chicken. Cover and cook on low setting for 4 to 6 hours, until chicken is no longer pink inside. To serve, remove toothpicks and arrange chicken rolls on serving plate; spoon sauce from slow cooker over rolls.

Pita halves are perfect for slow-cooker sandwich fillings...extra easy for little hands to hold without spills!

Greek Chicken Pitas

Serves 4

1 onion, diced
3 cloves garlic, minced
1 lb. boneless, skinless chicken
    breasts, cut into strips
1 t. lemon-pepper seasoning
1/2 t. dried oregano
1/4 t. allspice

1/4 c. plain yogurt
1/4 c. sour cream
1/2 c. cucumber, peeled
    and diced
4 rounds pita bread, halved
    and split

Place onion and garlic in a slow cooker; set aside. Sprinkle chicken with seasonings; place in a slow cooker. Cover and cook on low setting for 4 to 6 hours. Stir together yogurt, sour cream and cucumber in a small bowl; chill. Fill pita halves with chicken and drizzle with yogurt sauce.

Rolls and buns will drip less when filled with juicy slow-cooked meat if they're toasted first.

Creamy Chicken Sandwiches

Serves 8 to 10

2 12-oz. cans chicken, drained
10-3/4 oz. can cream of
    chicken soup
10-3/4 oz. can cream of
    mushroom soup

1 t. garlic powder
pepper to taste
1 c. potato chips, coarsely
    crushed
8 to 10 buns, split

Mix together chicken and soups; add seasonings and crushed chips.
Spoon into a slow cooker; cover and cook on high setting for 4 hours.
Serve on buns.

Stews, chowders and cream soups are perfect comfort foods.
Make yours extra creamy and rich tasting...simply replace milk or
water in the recipe with an equal amount of evaporated milk.

Chicken Stew & Dumplings

Serves 4 to 6

3 onions, quartered
3 stalks celery, cut into 1-inch
    pieces
1 T. butter
3 to 4-lb. chicken
3 c. chicken broth
16-oz. pkg. carrots, peeled and
    cut into 1-inch pieces

1 bay leaf
salt and pepper to taste
2 T. all-purpose flour
1/4 c. cold water
2 c. biscuit baking mix
2/3 c. milk

In a Dutch oven, sauté onions and celery in butter over medium heat until tender. Add chicken and sauté until golden on all sides. Stir in broth, carrots, bay leaf, salt and pepper. Cover and simmer over low heat for 2 hours, stirring occasionally. Remove chicken from pan; remove and discard skin. Pull meat from bones; return to Dutch oven. Mix flour and water; add to stew. In a bowl, combine baking mix and milk. Drop by tablespoonfuls into simmering stew. Cook, uncovered, for 10 minutes. Cover and cook for an additional 10 minutes. Discard bay leaf before serving.

Worries go down better with soup.

-Old Yiddish Proverb

Chicken Pot Pie Soup

Serves 8 to 10

1-1/2 c. butter
1-1/2 c. all-purpose flour
4 t. salt
1/2 t. pepper
2 pts. half-and-half
6 c. seasoned chicken broth

6 boneless, skinless chicken
    breasts, cooked and cubed
5 to 6 potatoes, peeled, cubed
    and cooked
3 c. mixed vegetables

Melt butter in a large Dutch oven over medium heat; whisk in flour, salt and pepper. Heat and stir over low heat until smooth and bubbly; remove from heat. Carefully whisk in half-and-half and broth; return to heat and bring to a boil. Reduce heat; add remaining ingredients. Simmer until vegetables are tender.

Buying boneless, skinless chicken breasts in bulk? Cook them all at once. Season with salt, pepper and garlic, if desired, and allow to cool. Wrap tightly in plastic or place in a freezer bag. Kept in the freezer, they'll be ready for quick lunches, sandwiches or even zesty fajitas!

Chicken Soup Au Gratin

Serves 4 to 6

2 boneless, skinless chicken
    breasts
2 c. water
1/2 t. salt
1/2 c. onion, chopped
1/2 c. carrots, peeled and
    chopped
1/2 c. celery, chopped
10-3/4 oz. can cream of chicken
    soup
1/2 c. milk
1/8 t. pepper
1 c. shredded Cheddar cheese

Combine chicken, water and salt in a large saucepan over medium
heat; simmer until tender. Remove chicken, reserving broth in
saucepan; let chicken cool, then dice and set aside. Add vegetables to
broth in pan; simmer until tender. Stir in soup, milk and pepper; add
cheese and chicken. Heat through, stirring until cheese melts.

Pour soup samples into a variety of thermoses and let
guests help themselves. The soup will stay nice and warm
and the thermoses can be tucked into a picnic basket
for easy toting to and from supper.

Chicken Chili with Green Salsa

Serves 4

1 T. oil
12-oz. pkg. chicken breast
    tenders, cut into 1/2-inch
    strips
2 15-1/2 oz. cans white kidney
    beans, drained and rinsed

16-oz. jar mild green salsa
1/4 c. fresh cilantro, chopped
1/2 c. water
Optional: cherry tomatoes,
    quartered

Heat oil in a skillet over medium heat. Sauté chicken for 2 to
3 minutes, until juices run clear when pierced with a fork. Add
beans, salsa, cilantro and water. Cook for about 5 minutes, until
heated through. Ladle into serving bowls; top with tomatoes,
if desired.

Need to feed a few extra guests? It's easy to
stretch soup! Some quick-cooking add-ins are orzo pasta,
ramen noodles, instant rice or canned beans. Simmer for
just a few minutes until heated through.

Chicken Tortilla Soup

Serves 6

14-1/2 oz. can chicken broth
10-3/4 oz. cream of chicken
    soup
15-1/2 oz. can black beans,
    drained and rinsed
14-oz. can sweet corn & diced
    peppers, drained

10-oz. can tomatoes with chiles
12-oz. can chicken, drained
8-oz. pkg. pasteurized process
    cheese spread, diced

Combine all ingredients except cheese in a stockpot over medium-low heat. Simmer until heated through. Stir in cheese until melted.

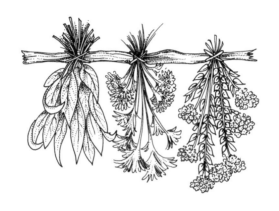

Try drying fresh herbs from your garden...it's so easy! Simply cut bunches and tie with jute, then hang on a peg rack. The herbs will dry naturally and lend a country look to your kitchen. Pinch off sprigs to add flavor to recipes.

Chicken & Herb Soup

Serves 4

1 onion, chopped
1 sweet onion, chopped
4 shallots, chopped
1/4 c. butter
1 T. olive oil
2 14-1/2 oz. cans chicken broth

1/2 t. ground cumin
1 t. dried oregano
1/2 t. dried thyme
Optional: 3 T. dry white wine
10-oz. can chicken, drained
8-oz. container plain yogurt

In a Dutch oven, sauté onions and shallots in butter and olive oil over low heat. Cook until tender; add broth, cumin, oregano and thyme. Bring to a boil over medium heat; reduce heat and simmer for 20 minutes, stirring frequently. Add wine, if desired; simmer for an additional 20 minutes, stirring often. Pour mixture into a blender and process until smooth; return to Dutch oven. Stir in chicken; heat through. Add yogurt blending until smooth and creamy; serve immediately.

Ahhh, soup & bread! Stop by the bakery for a fresh loaf of bread. Warmed slightly in the oven and topped with real butter, it's heavenly with any dinner!

Spinach-Chicken Noodle Soup

Serves 6 to 8

4 14-1/2 oz. cans chicken broth
1 c. onions, chopped
1 c. carrots, peeled and sliced
2 10-3/4 oz. cans cream of
   chicken soup
10-oz. pkg. frozen chopped
   spinach, thawed

4 c. cooked chicken, chopped
2 c. medium egg noodles,
   uncooked
1/2 t. salt
1/2 t. pepper

Combine broth, onions and carrots in a Dutch oven. Bring to a
boil over medium-high heat. Reduce heat, cover and simmer for
15 minutes. Add remaining ingredients. Bring to a boil, reduce heat
and simmer, uncovered, for an additional 15 minutes.

Wrap up the ingredients for Quick & Easy Chicken Noodle Soup in a basket with a big napkin and deliver to someone who's under the weather...tie on the recipe with a raffia bow. How thoughtful!

Quick & Easy Chicken Noodle Soup

Serves 8 to 10

10 c. water
10 cubes chicken bouillon
2 10-1/2 oz. cans chicken,
   drained
10-3/4 oz. can cream of
   chicken soup

10-3/4 oz. can cream of
   celery soup
1-1/2 oz. pkg. onion soup mix
8-oz. pkg. wide egg noodles,
   uncooked

Bring water to a boil in a stockpot; add bouillon cubes and boil until dissolved. Add chicken, soups and soup mix; return to a boil over medium heat. Stir in noodles; bring to a boil. Reduce heat and simmer until noodles are tender, 8 to 10 minutes.

Serve up stew in mugs lined with homemade herbed croutons. Cut out fun shapes from sliced bread, brush with butter, sprinkle with herbs and bake at 200 degrees until golden and crisp.

Chicken & Barley Stew

Serves 6 to 8

1/4 c. butter
2 T. all-purpose flour
2-1/2 c. water
3 cubes chicken bouillon
2 boneless, skinless chicken
   breasts, cubed
1/2 c. pearled barley, uncooked
2 carrots, peeled and sliced
2 stalks celery, sliced

2 T. dried thyme
20 cherry tomatoes
4-oz. can whole mushrooms,
   drained
1 bunch green onions, sliced
1/8 t. browning and seasoning
   sauce
salt and pepper to taste

Melt butter over low heat in a large stockpot; stir in flour. Gradually stir in water and bouillon cubes, stirring constantly. Add chicken, barley, carrots, celery and thyme. Simmer over medium heat for 30 minutes, stirring frequently. Add remaining ingredients; reduce heat to low. Simmer for 2 additional hours, stirring occasionally. Crush tomatoes with a spoon before serving.

Save extra broth by freezing in an ice cube tray or muffin tin. Add the broth cubes when cooking rice or veggies...a real flavor boost.

Chicken Corn Chowder

Serves 6 to 8

1-1/2 c. milk
10-1/2 oz. can chicken broth
10-3/4 oz. can cream of
    chicken soup
10-3/4 oz. can cream of
    potato soup
2 10-oz. cans chicken, drained

1/3 c. green onion, chopped
11-oz. can sweet corn & diced
    peppers
4-oz. can chopped green chiles,
    drained
8-oz. pkg. shredded Cheddar
    cheese

Combine all ingredients except cheese in a stockpot. Heat over low heat, stirring frequently, for about 15 minutes, until heated through. Add cheese; stir until melted.

No Cajun seasoning on hand? Mix together 1/2 teaspoon black
pepper, 1/2 teaspoon white pepper, 1/2 teaspoon garlic powder,
1/2 teaspoon onion powder, 1/2 teaspoon cayenne
pepper and 1/2 teaspoon paprika.

South Carolina Gumbo

Serves 6

2 boneless, skinless chicken
  breasts, cubed
2 c. okra, chopped
2 14-1/2 oz. cans chicken broth
1 c. water
14-1/2 oz. can diced tomatoes
1 onion, chopped

1 stalk celery, sliced
1/2 green pepper, chopped
1/4 t. garlic powder
1 t. Cajun seasoning
salt and pepper to taste
1 c. instant rice, uncooked

Combine all ingredients except rice in a stockpot; bring to a boil over
medium-high heat. Reduce heat and simmer, covered, for 15 minutes,
or until juices from chicken run clear when pierced with fork. Add rice;
simmer for 15 additional minutes.

In my grandmother's house there was always chicken soup
And talk of the old country...

–Louis Simpson

Chicken & Wild Rice Soup

Serves 6

2 c. cooked chicken, diced
6-oz. pkg. long-grain and wild
    rice, cooked
2 10-3/4 oz. cans cream of
    mushroom soup
10-3/4 oz. can cream of
    celery soup

14-1/2 oz. can chicken broth
Optional: 2 T. sherry
1 carrot, peeled and shredded
1 c. sliced mushrooms
1 pt. half-and-half

Combine all ingredients except half-and-half in a large stockpot; heat over medium heat until vegetables are tender. Reduce heat to low; gradually stir in half-and-half, heating through without boiling, about 30 minutes.

Cubed, cooked chicken can be purchased in vacuum-sealed foil pouches...just open and use in your favorite recipe.

Chicken Tortellini Soup

Serves 6

1 lb. boneless, skinless chicken
    breasts, cooked and cubed
9-oz. pkg. cheese tortellini,
    uncooked
46-oz. can chicken broth
1 c. carrots, peeled and chopped

1/2 c. onion, chopped
1/2 c. celery, sliced
1/2 t. dried thyme
1/4 t. pepper
1 bay leaf

Combine all ingredients in a stockpot; bring to a boil over medium heat. Reduce heat, cover and simmer until tortellini is tender. Discard bay leaf.

INDEX

INDEX

Our Story

Back in 1984, we were next-door neighbors raising our families in the little town of Delaware, Ohio. We were two moms with small children looking for a way to do what we loved and stay home with the kids too. We shared a love of home cooking and making memories with family & friends. After many a conversation over the backyard fence, **Gooseberry Patch** was born.

We put together the first catalog & cookbooks at our kitchen tables and packed boxes from the basement, enlisting the help of our loved ones wherever we could. From that little family, we've grown to include an amazing group of creative folks who love cooking, decorating and creating as much as we do.

Hard to believe it's been over 25 years since those kitchen-table days. Today, we're best known for our homestyle, family-friendly cookbooks. We love hand-picking the recipes and are tickled to share our inspiration, ideas and more with you! One thing's for sure, we couldn't have done it without our friends all across the country. Whether you've been along for the ride from the beginning or are just discovering us, welcome to our family!

Vickie & Jo Ann

Want to hear the latest from **Gooseberry Patch**?
www.gooseberrypatch.com

Join Our Circle of Friends

VIDEOS

Read Our Blog

Find us on Facebook

Follow us on twitter

1·800·854·6673